DRAWING TUTORIALS

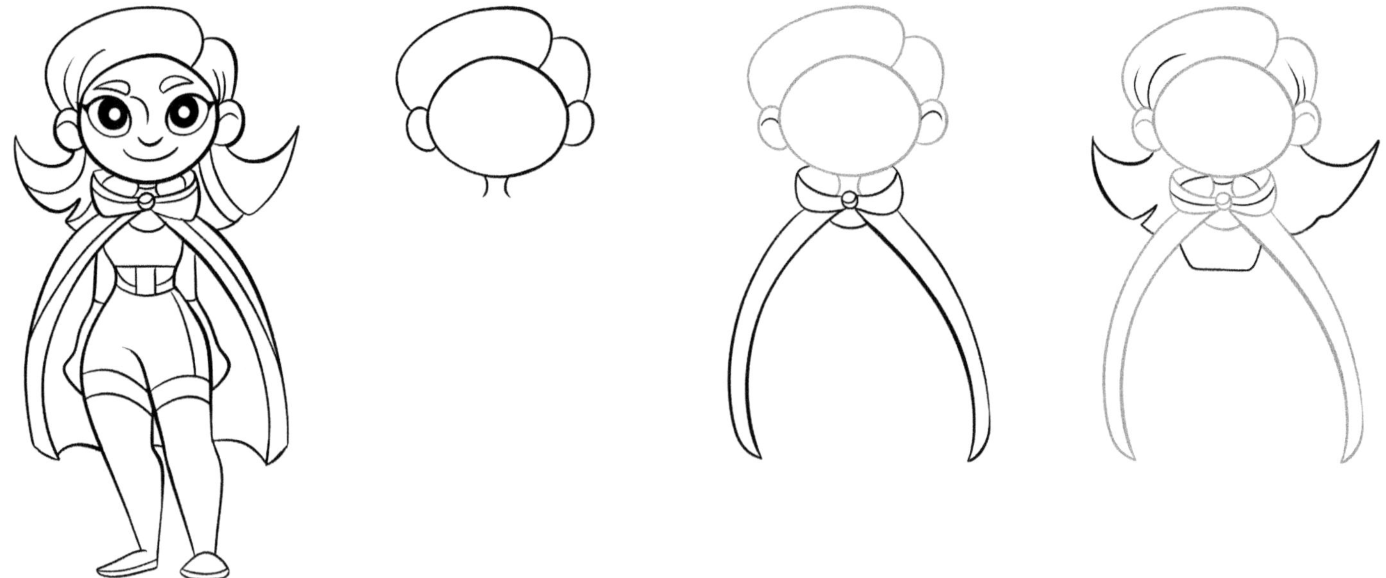

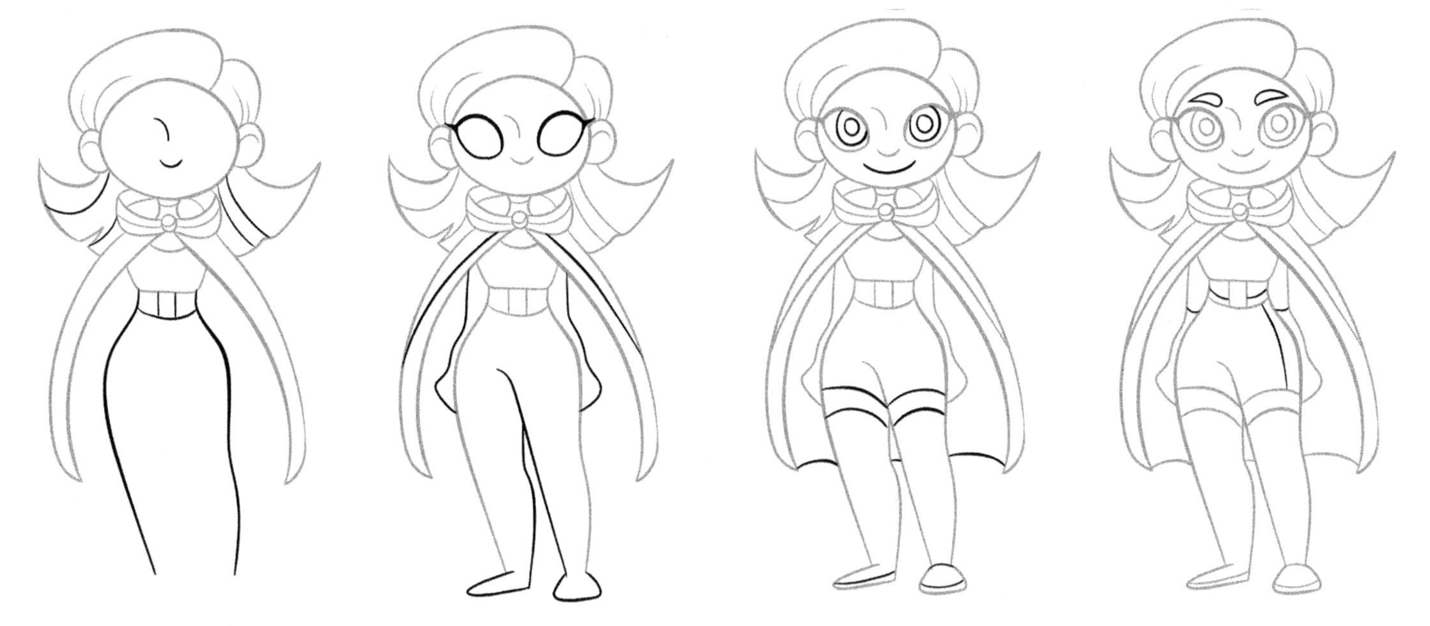

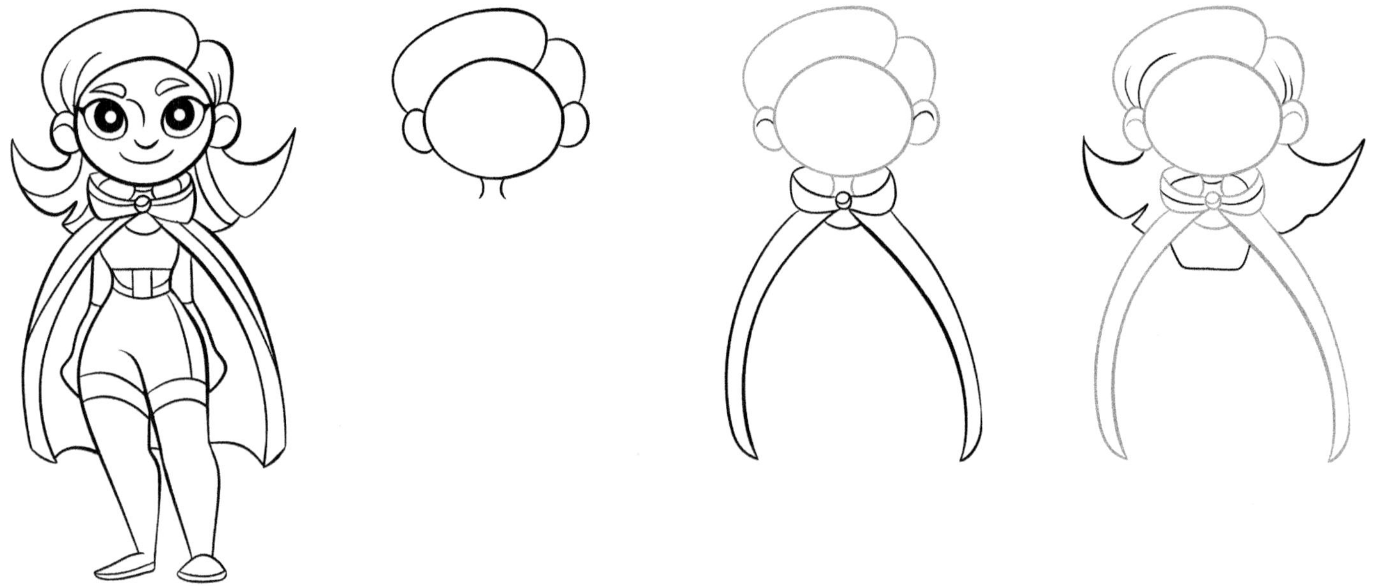

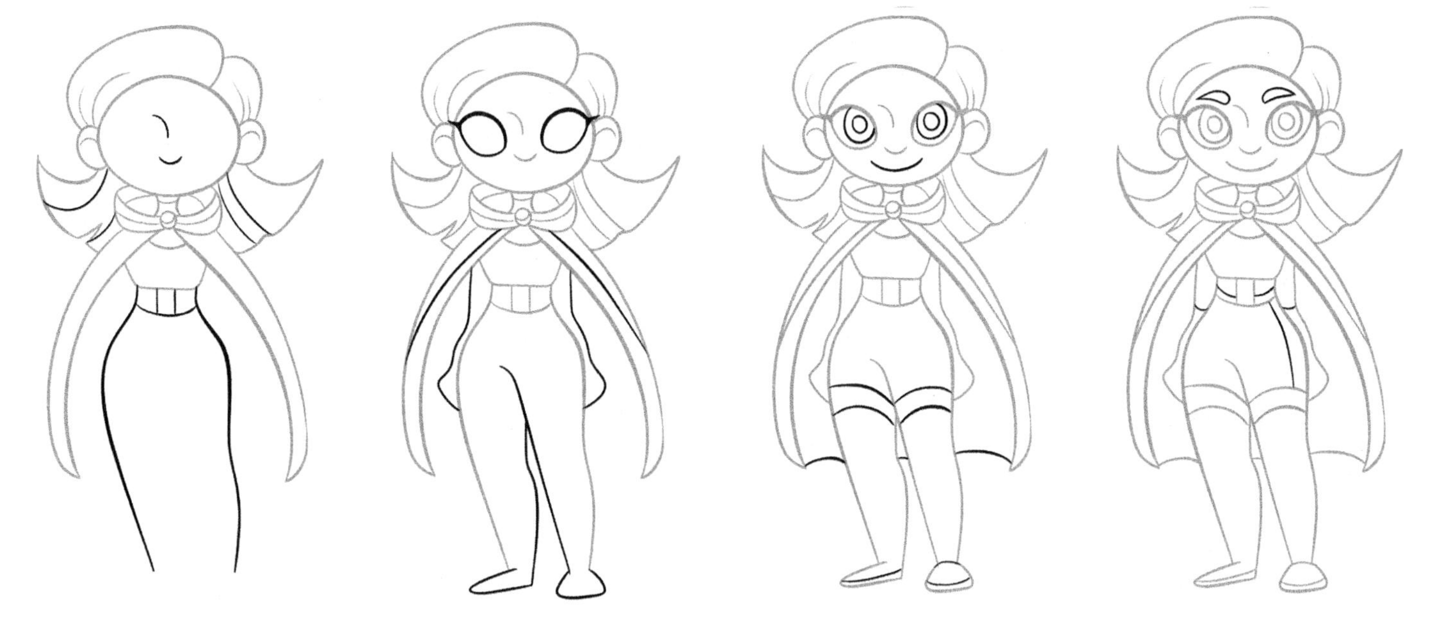

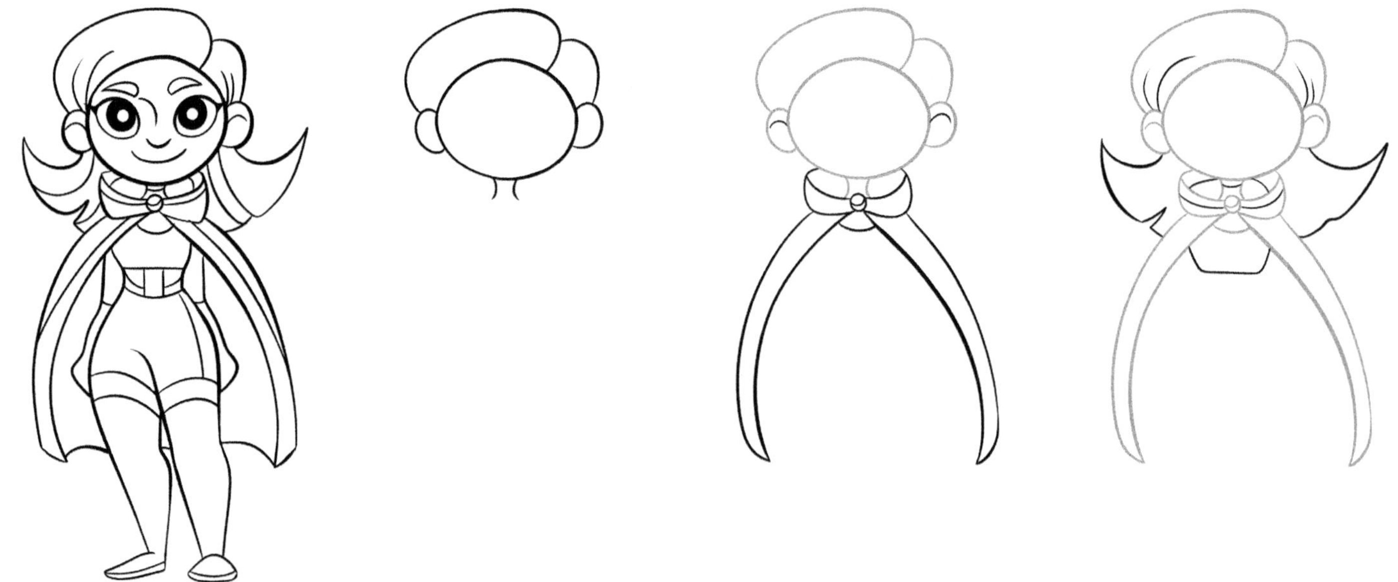

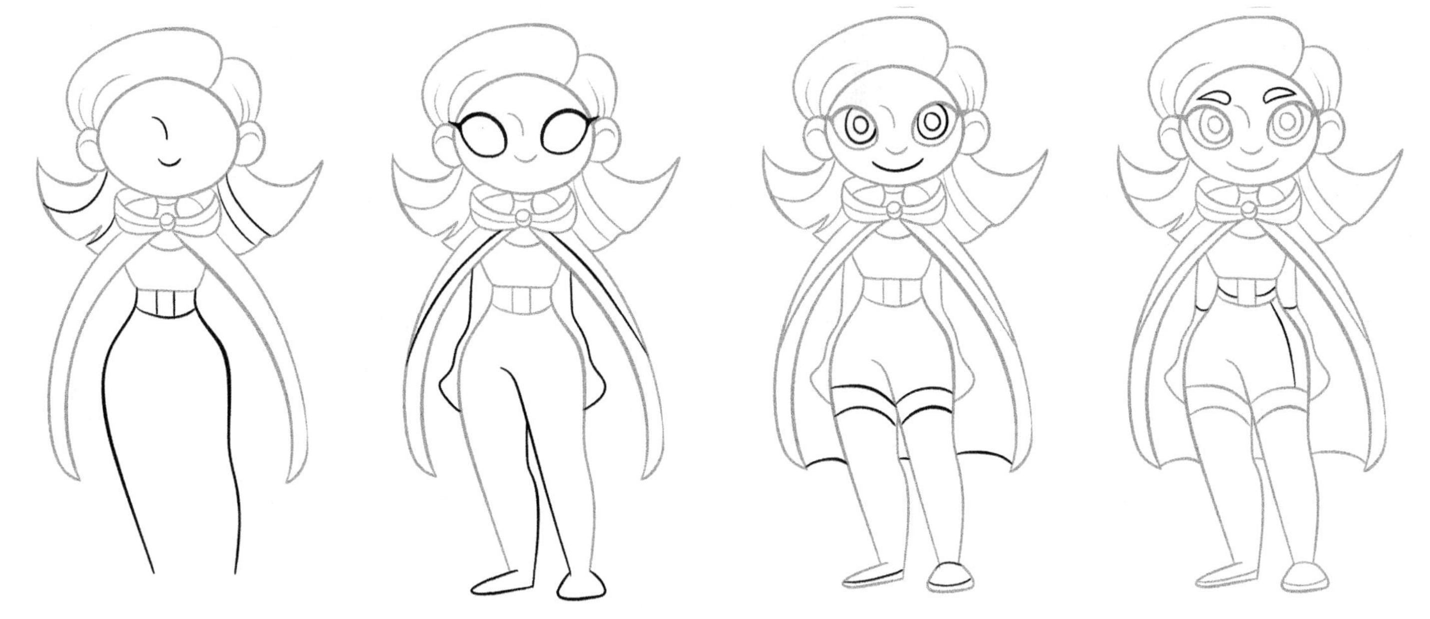

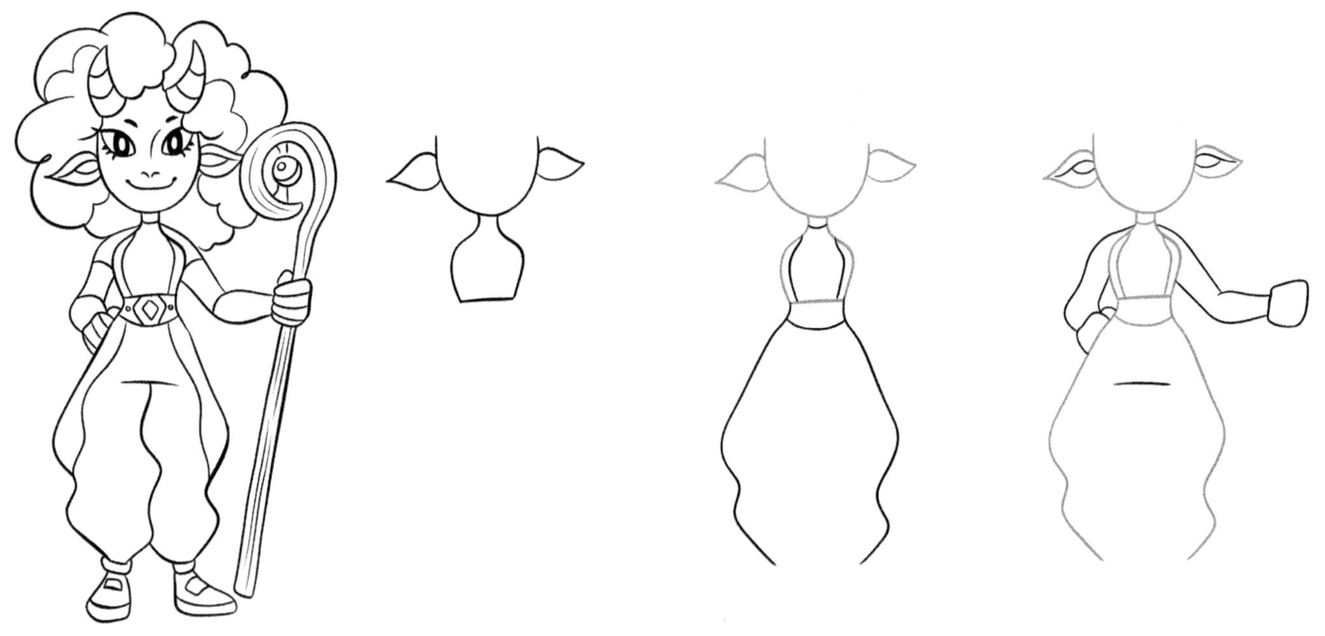

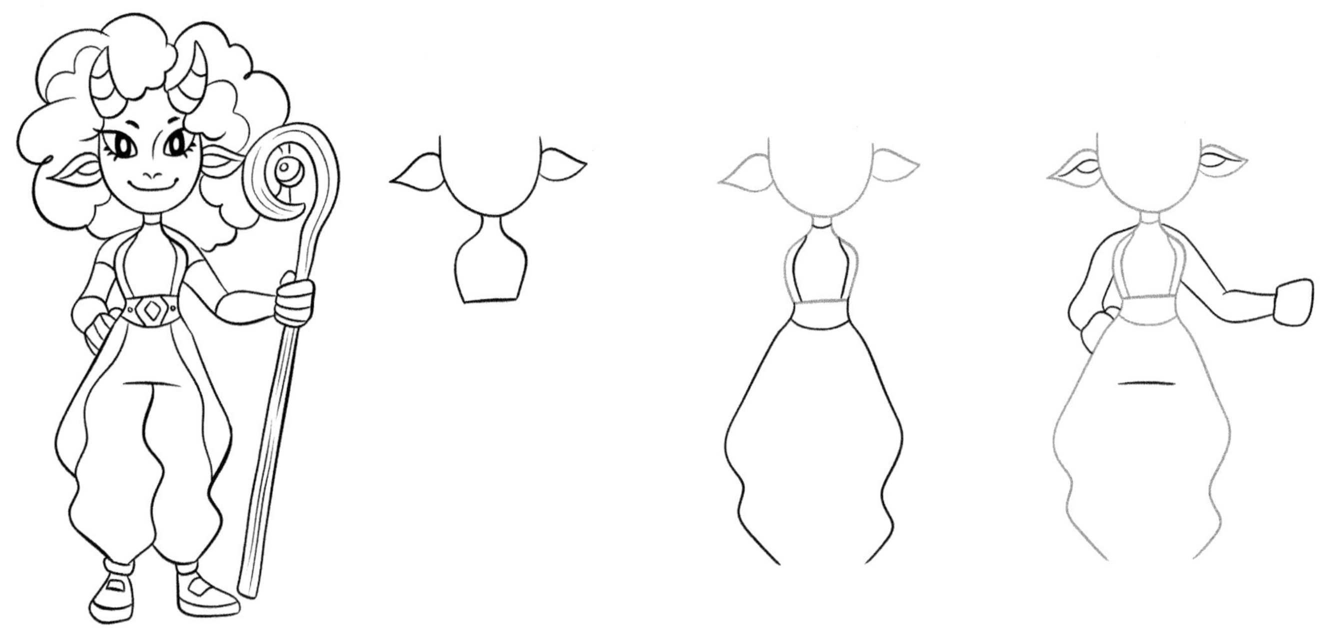

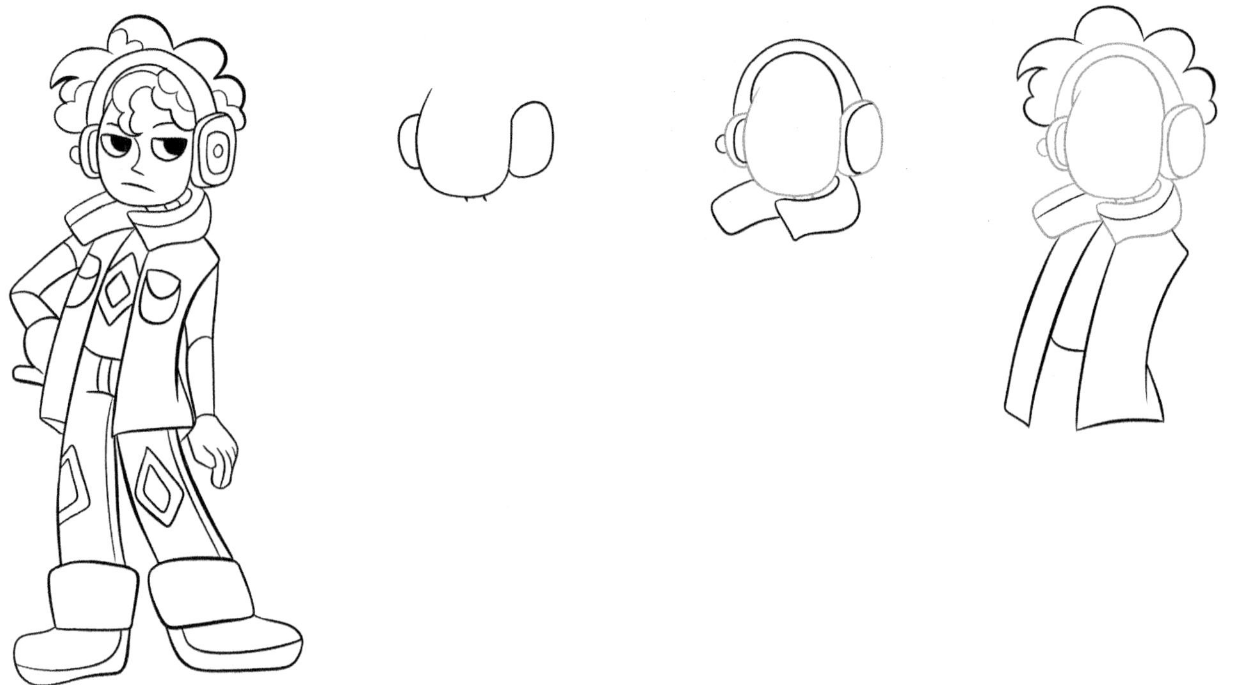

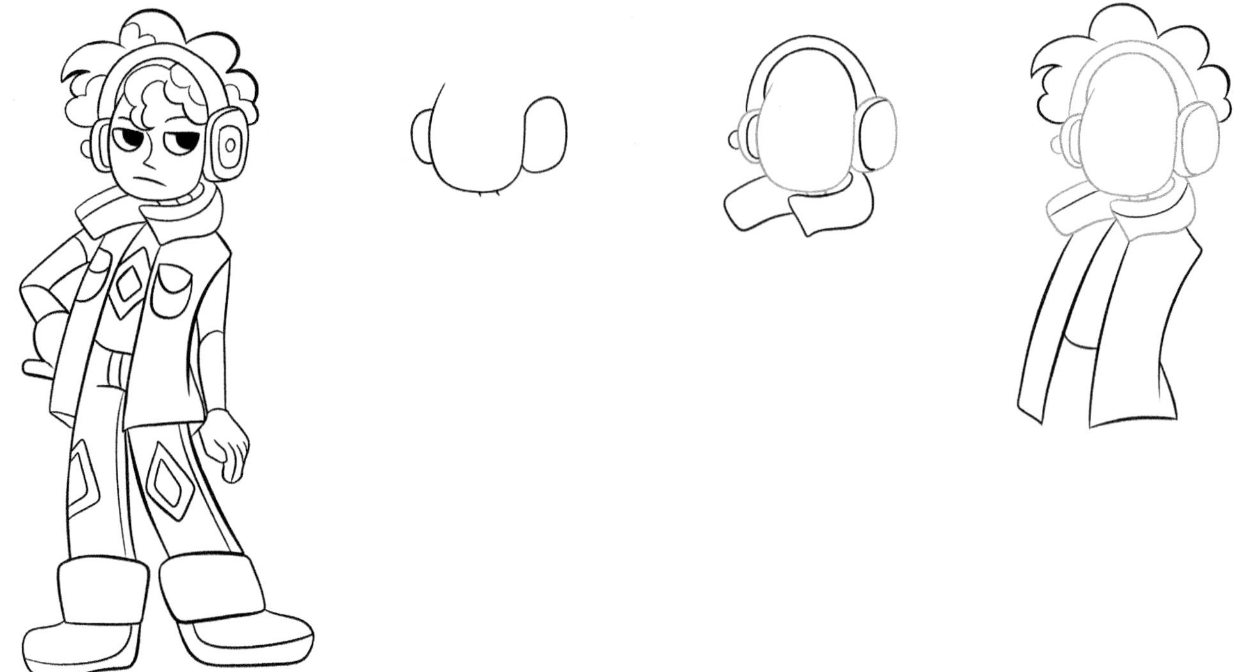

COLORING PAGES

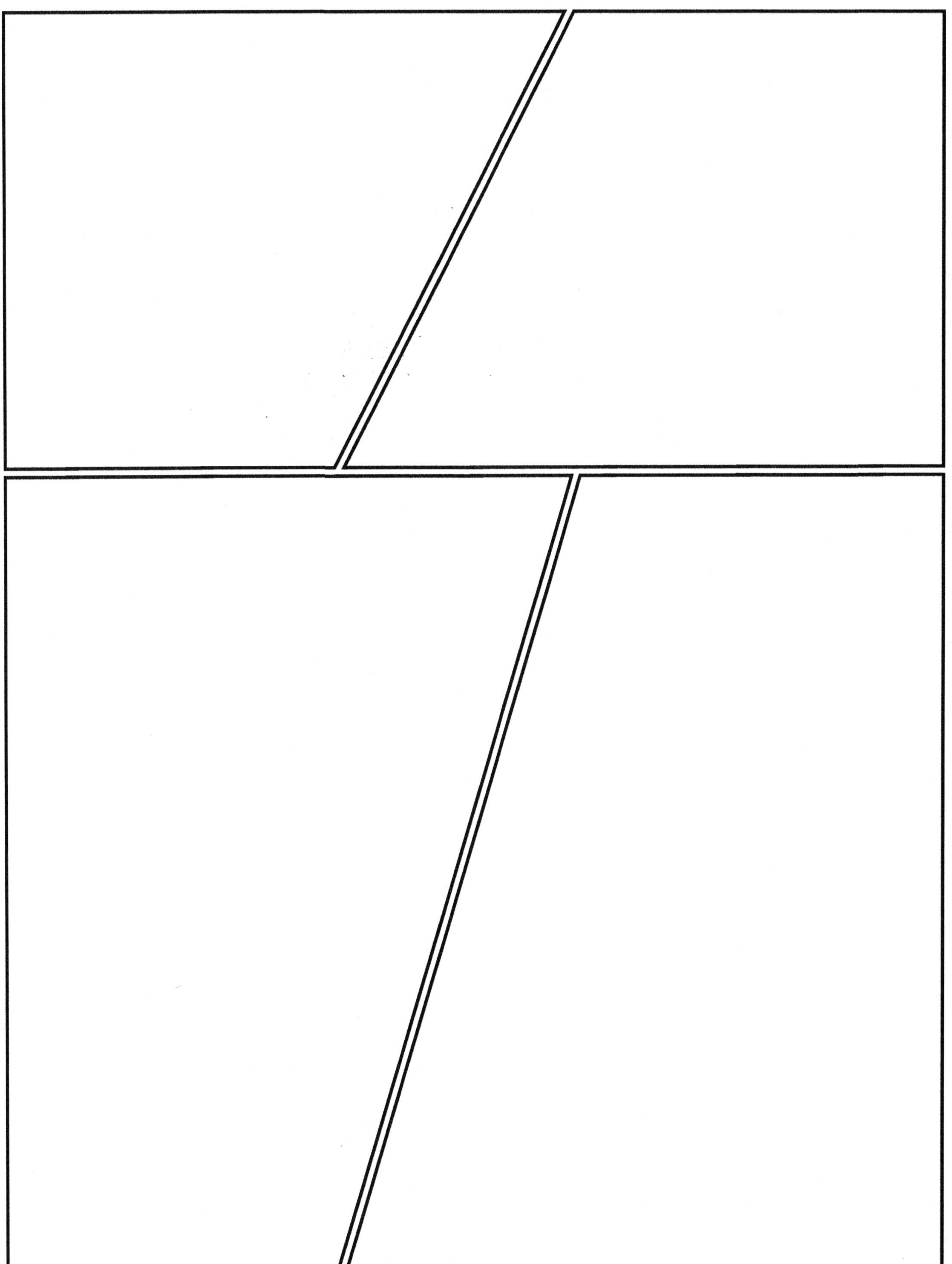

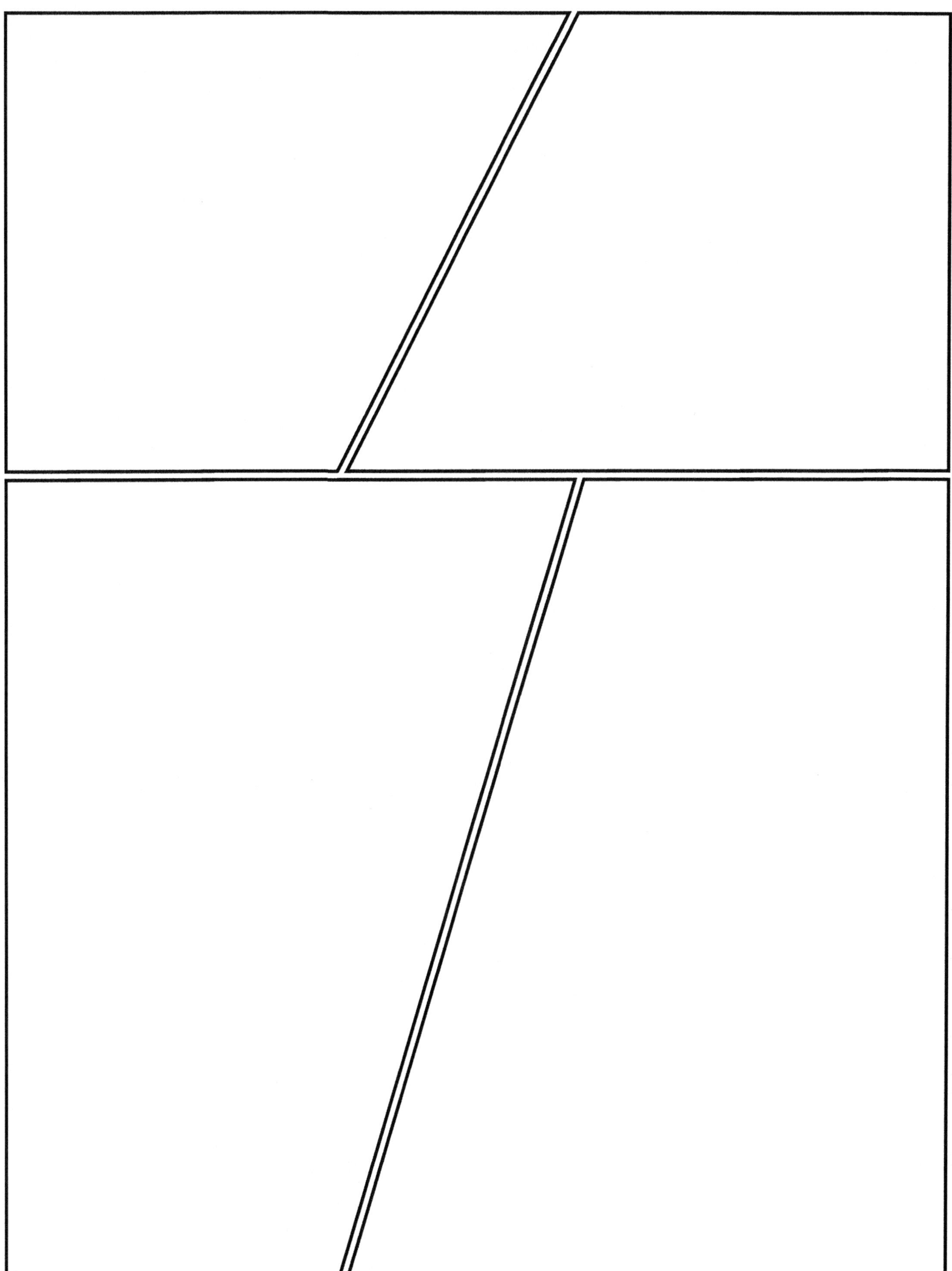

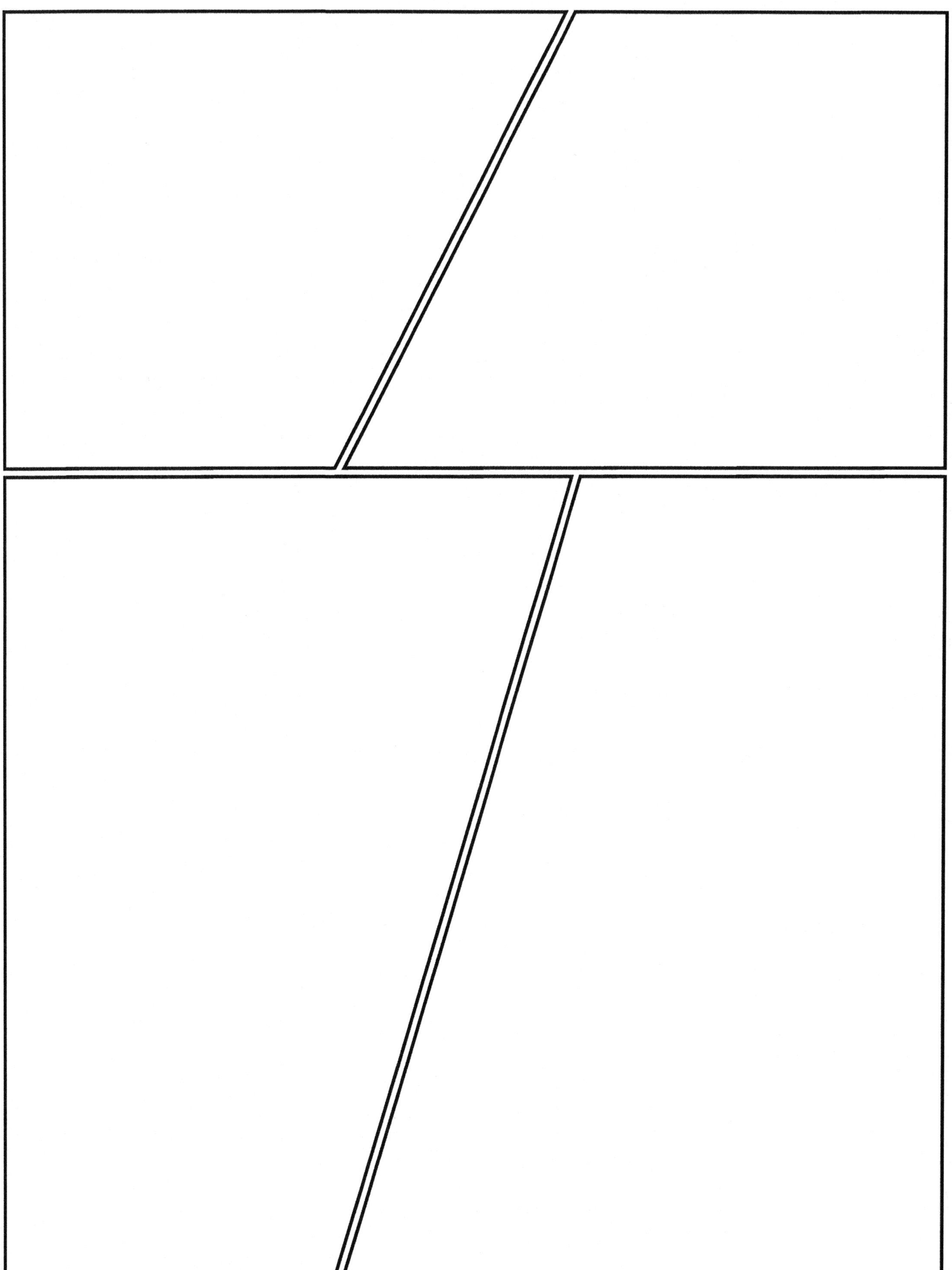

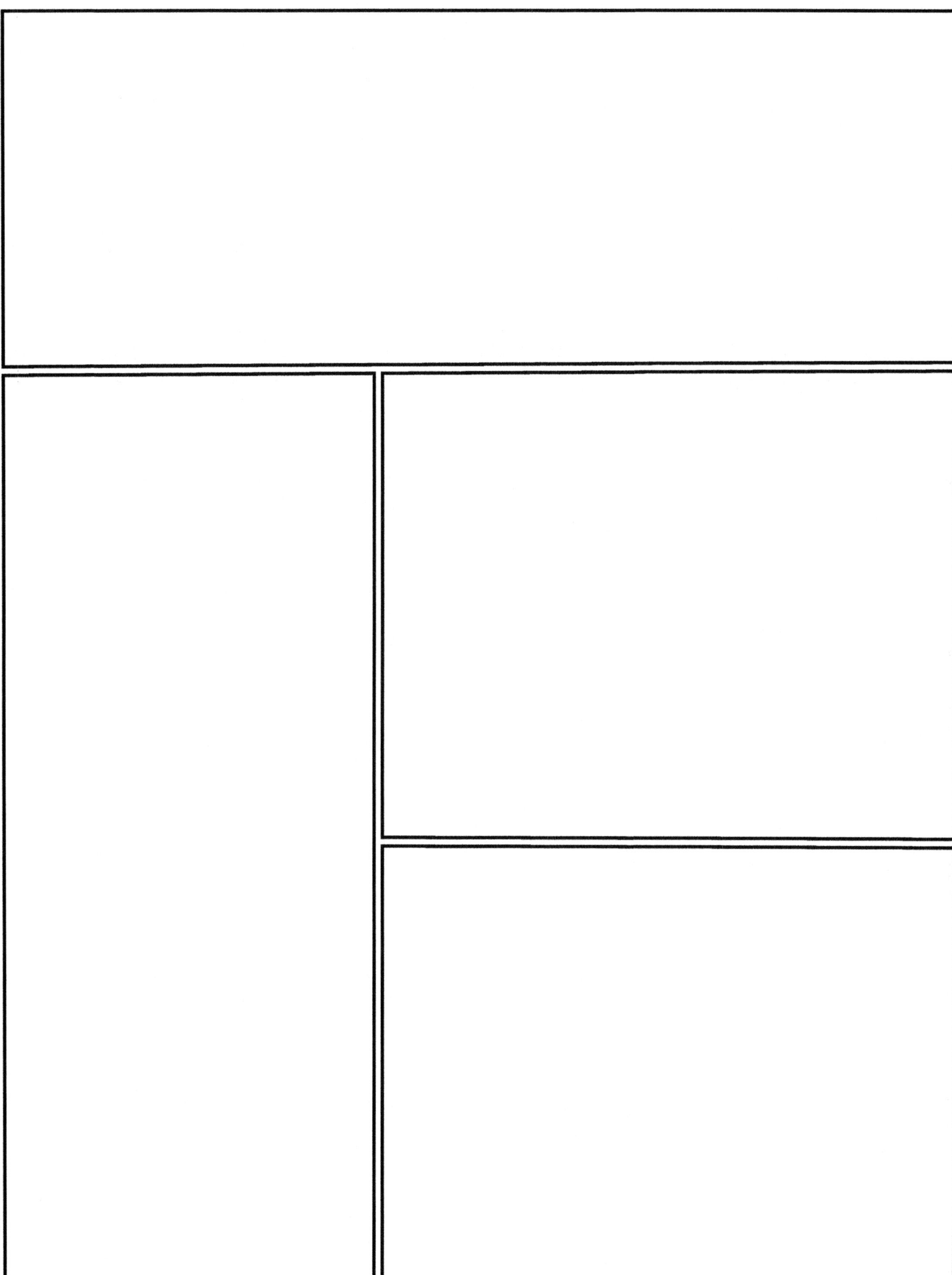

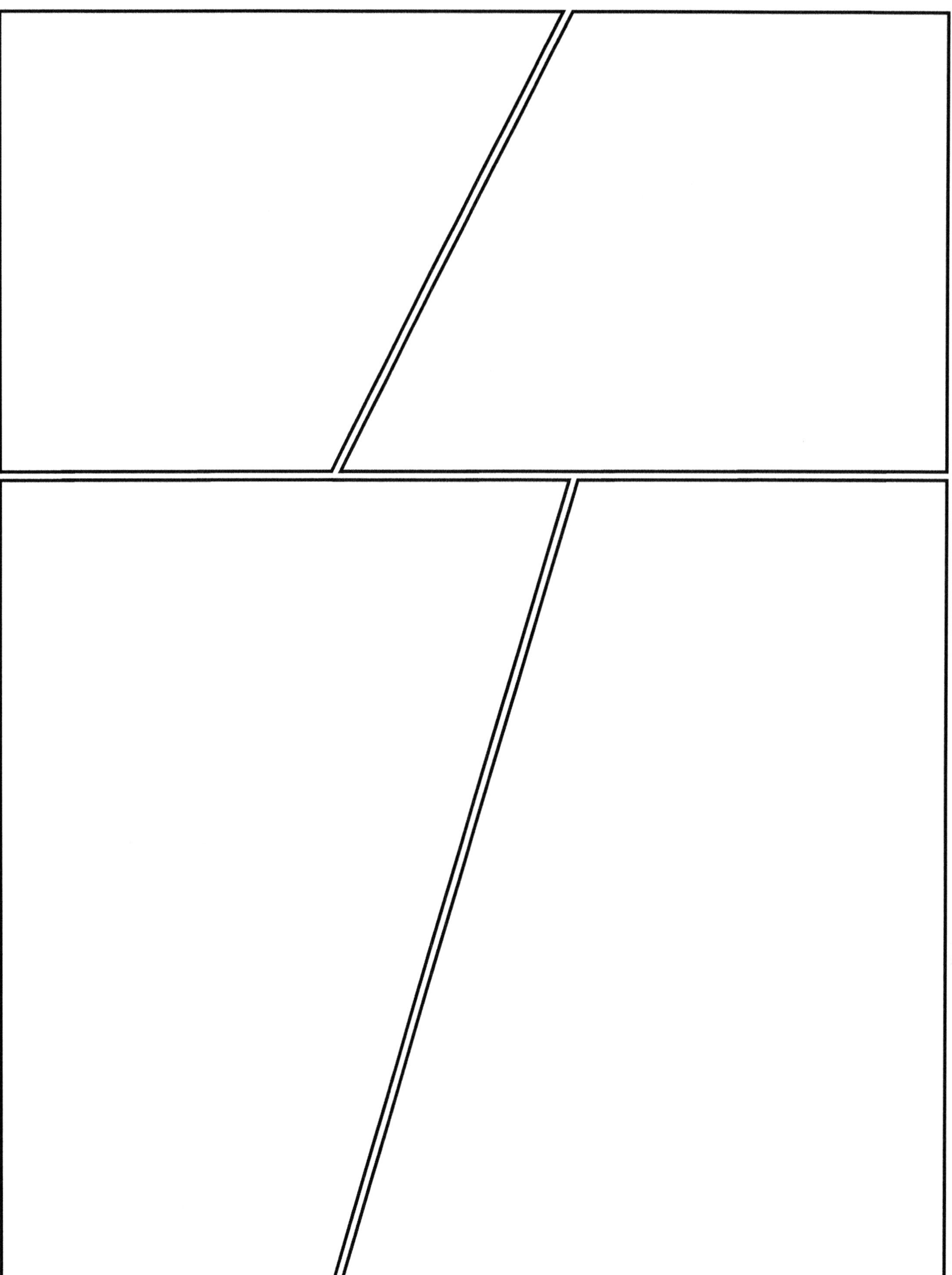

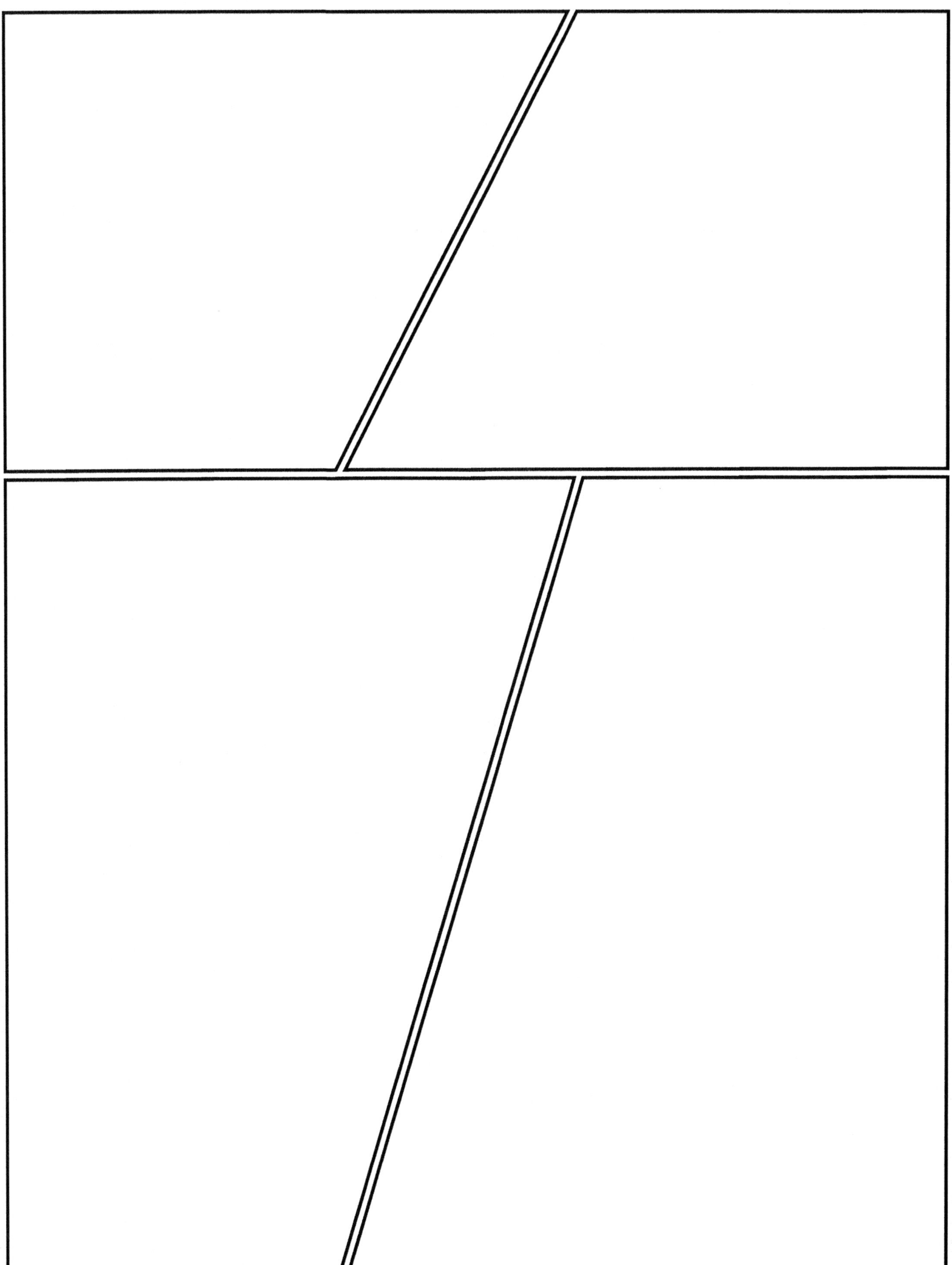

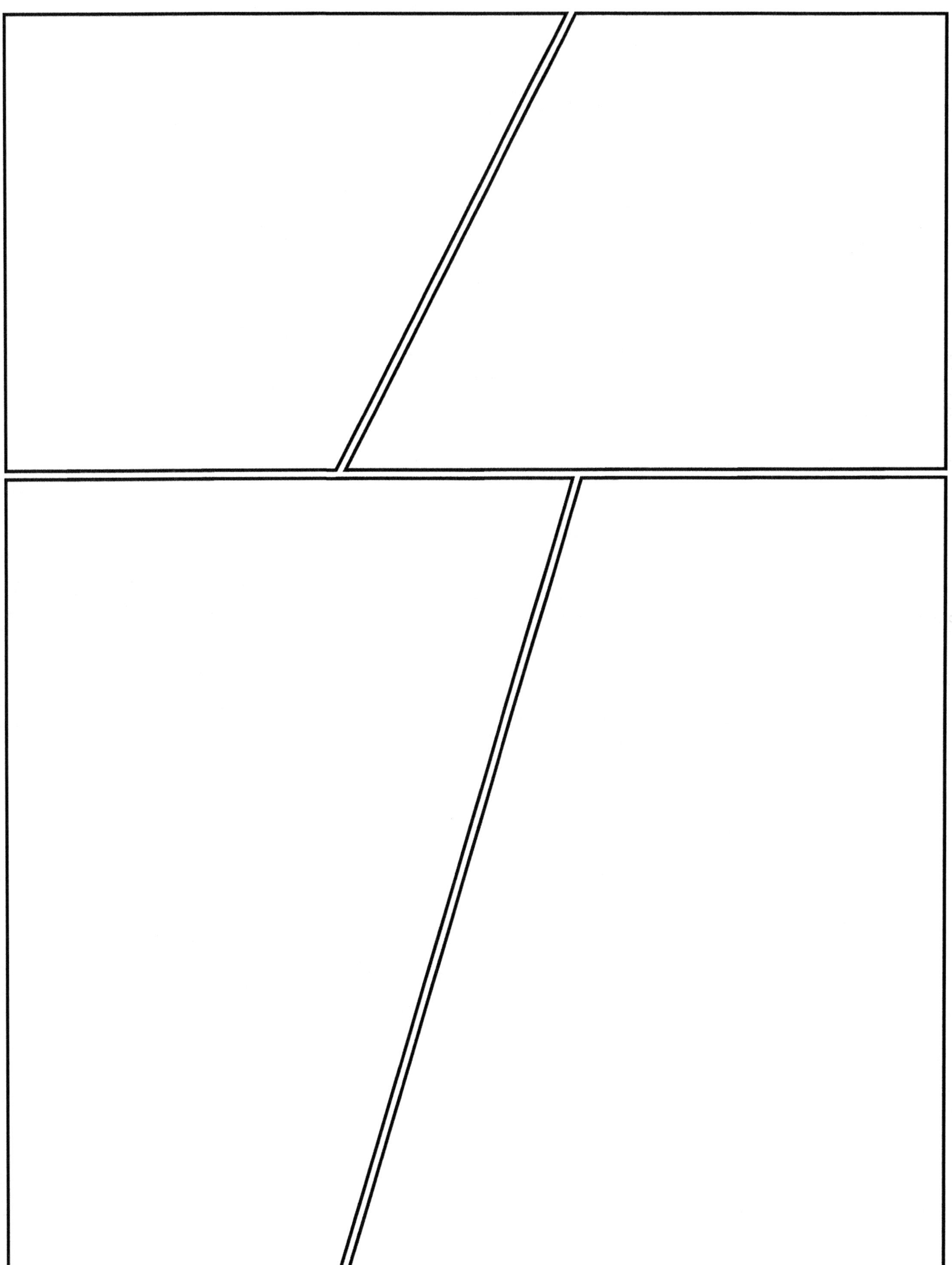

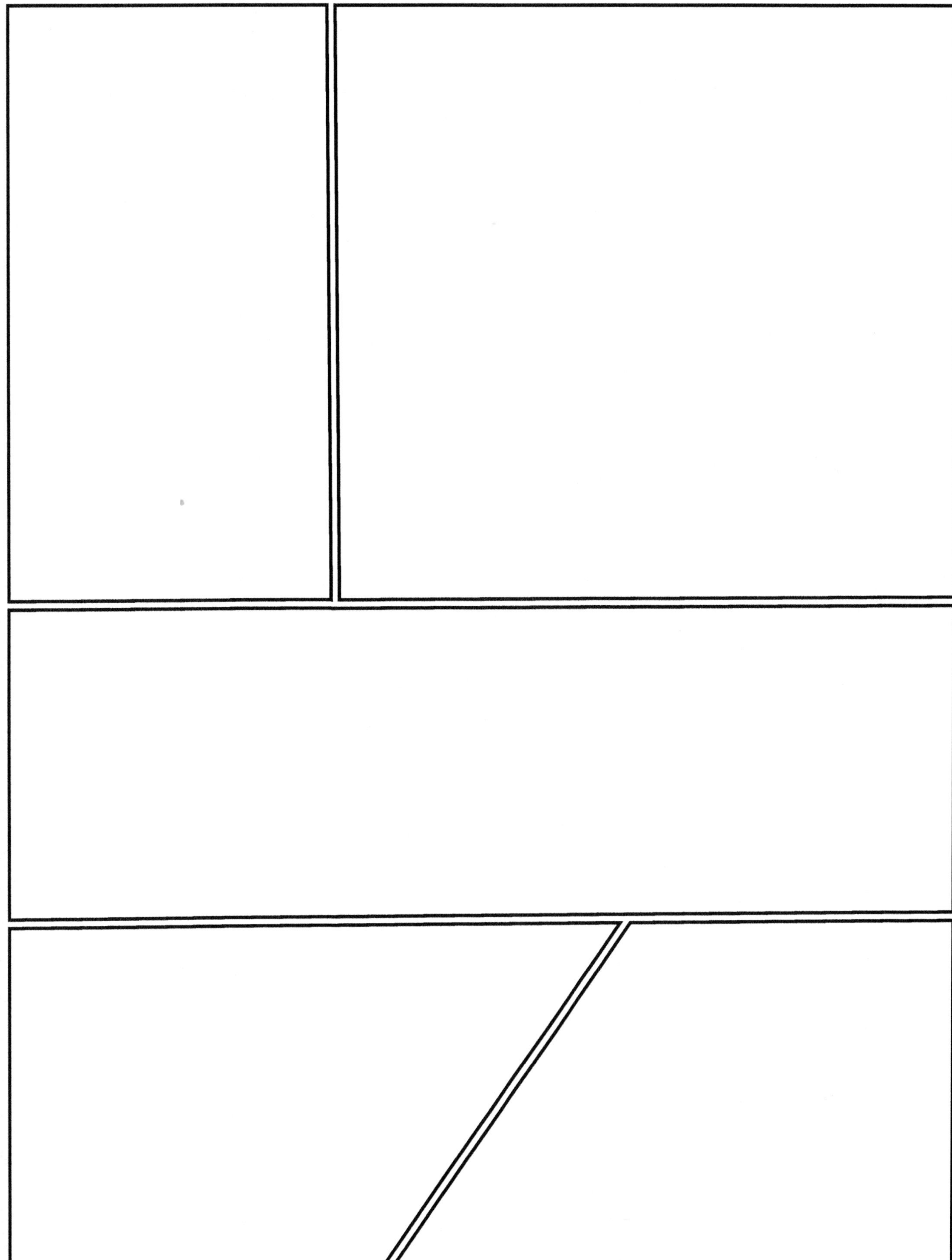

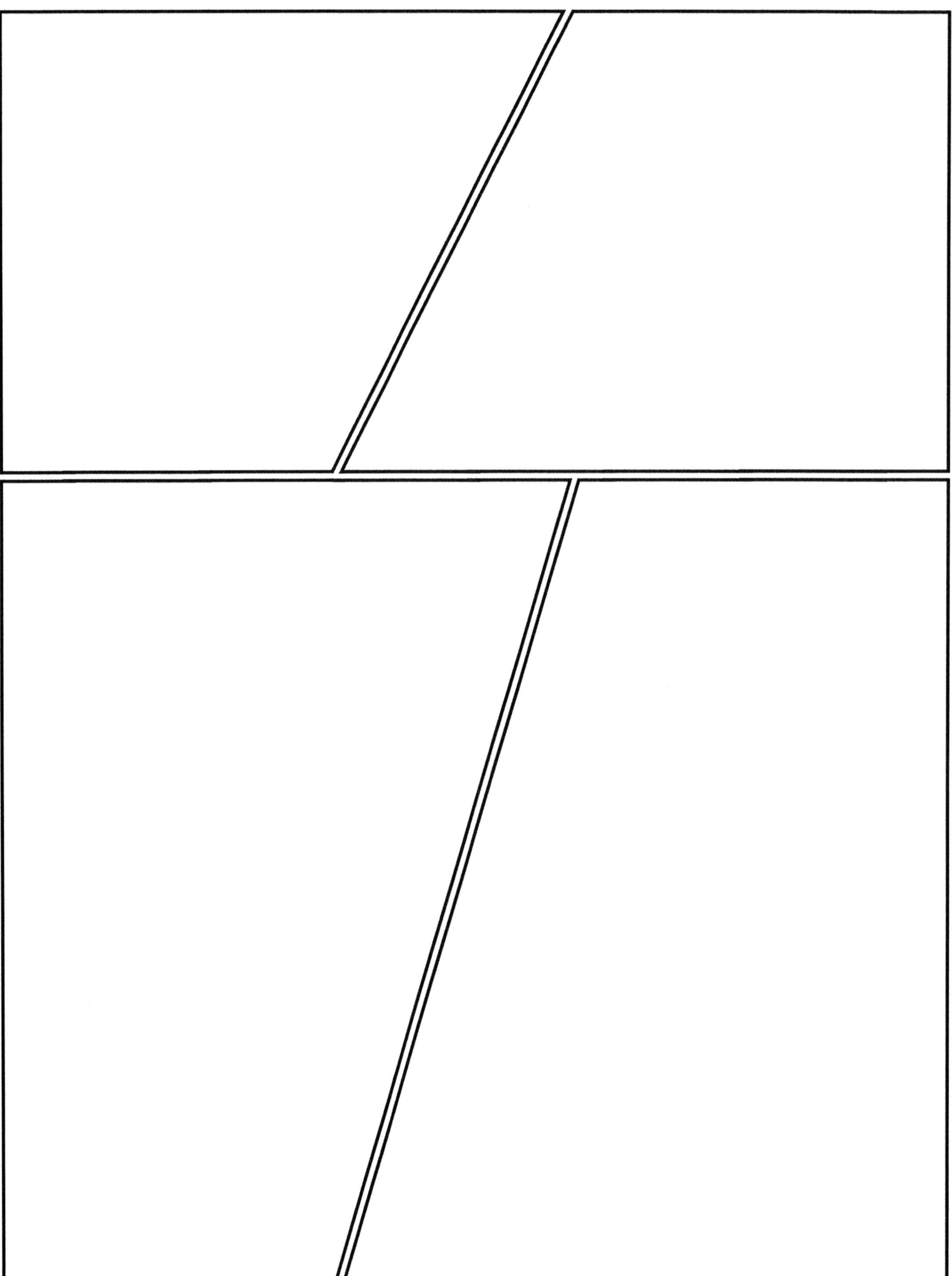

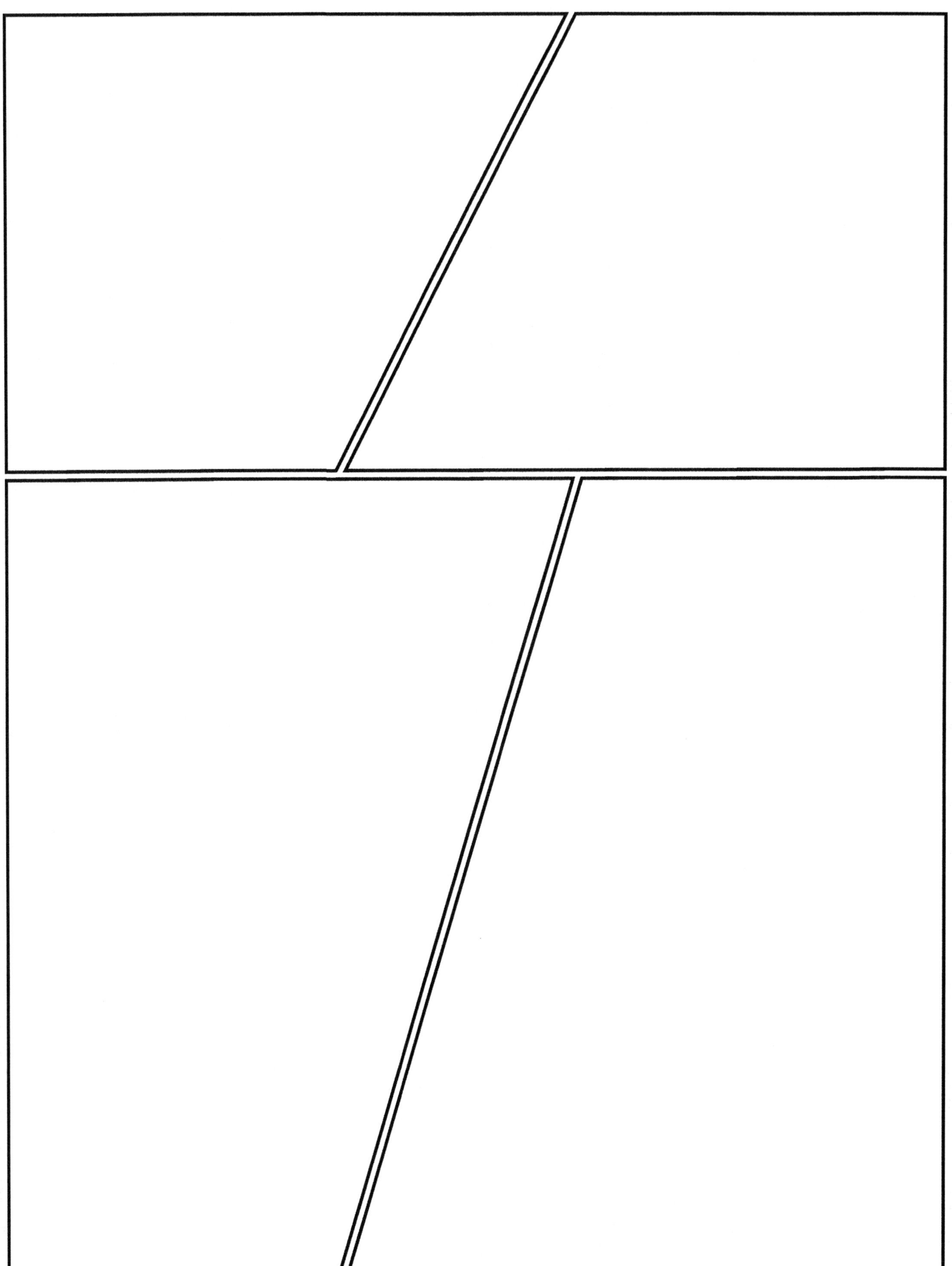

Printed in Great Britain
by Amazon

82562184R00059